D1549133

LOOK AT YOUR BODY

REPRODUCTION
AND
GROWTH

STEVE PARKER

ILLUSTRATED BY PETER BULL ASSOCIATES, AZIZ KHAN, AND IAN THOMPSON

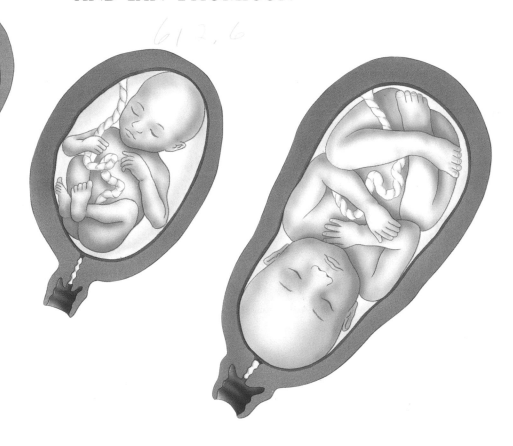

Copper Beech Books
Brookfield, Connecticut

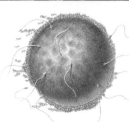
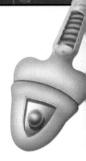

*First published in
the United States in 1998
by*
Copper Beech Books,
an imprint of
The Millbrook Press
2 Old New Milford Road
Brookfield, Connecticut
06804

Printed in Belgium

Editor
Jon Richards
Design
David West
Children's Book Design
Designer
Robert Perry
Illustrators
Peter Bull Associates,
Aziz Khan, and
Ian Thompson
Picture Research
Brooks Krikler Research
Consultant
Dr. Rachel Levene
MB.BS, DCH, DRCOG

Library of Congress
Cataloging-in-Publication Data
Parker, Steve.
Reproduction and growth / by Steve
Parker; illustrated by Ian Thompson.
    p. cm. — (Look at your body)
Includes index.
Summary: Presents an overview of the
human life cycle, with information
about reproduction, heredity, child
development, and aging.
ISBN 0-7613-0813-X (cblb)
    1. Human reproduction—
Juvenile literature. 2. Life cycle,
Human—Juvenile literature.
3. Embryology, Human—Juvenile
literature. [1. Life cycle, Human.
2. Reproduction. 3. Growth.]
I. Thompson, Ian, 1964- ill.
II. Title. III. Series.
QP251.5.P369 1998   97-43128
612.6—dc21   CIP AC

CONTENTS

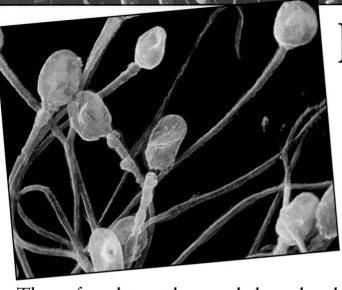

INTRODUCTION

LOOK AT YOUR BODY! Have you ever wondered how you got to be what you are today? At the very start of your life you began as two microscopically tiny cells. These fused together and then developed inside the safety of your mother's womb. Here, as the cells continued to divide and your tiny body formed, your mother supplied all of your nutrients to make sure that, when you were born, you came out as a fit, healthy baby.

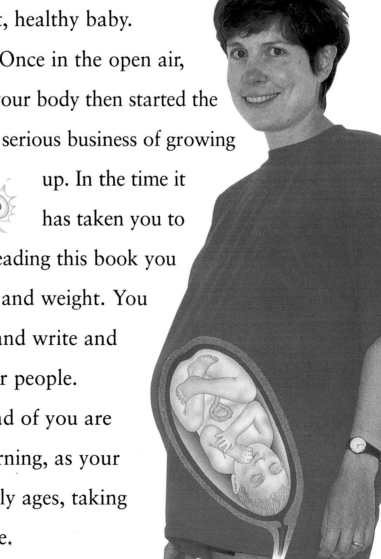

Once in the open air, your body then started the serious business of growing up. In the time it has taken you to get from birth to when you're reading this book you will have grown a lot in height and weight. You will have learned how to read and write and how to communicate with other people.

But it doesn't stop here. Ahead of you are many years of growing and learning, as your body matures and then gradually ages, taking you, with luck, to a ripe old age.

CYCLES of LIFE

LIFE HAS CONTINUED for hundreds, thousands, and even millions of years. But individual living things only live for a short time. They are born or hatched, grow up, grow old, and die. The reason that life continues is reproduction. Living things reproduce in a great many ways. Some simply split in two, or make copies of themselves — a method called asexual reproduction (*see below*). Others use a method of reproduction that involves two sexes. These two sexes, known as male and female, come together and mate to make offspring, using the sex organs of their reproductive system. This is known as sexual reproduction.

Petal

Stamen

Ovary

FLOWERS
A typical flower has both female parts and male parts. The male parts, called stamens, produce tiny grains, called pollen, which contain the male sex cells. The female parts contain the female sex cells, or tiny eggs, known as ovules. These ovules are stored inside the ovary (above).

4

INSECTS
Normally, insects reproduce sexually with two adults mating. However, under certain conditions female aphids (below) do not need males. They can produce offspring without mating. This is known as parthenogenesis.

ONE BECOMES TWO
Very small living things can reproduce in simple ways. Lying in the mud of a pond, the microscopic single-celled amoeba (above) simply splits, or divides, in two. This is called binary fission. Each "daughter" cell grows larger, and then splits again in the same way. Since there is no partner or sex involved, this is called asexual reproduction.

EGGS
Humans and other mammals (see below) are unusual in the animal world. They give birth — the female produces fully-formed young from her body. In the vast majority of animals, females do not give birth to babies, but lay eggs. The babies develop inside the eggs and then hatch out. The eggs of reptiles, such as crocodiles (right) and birds, are protected by a tough outer shell. Inside, the baby grows with its own store of food.

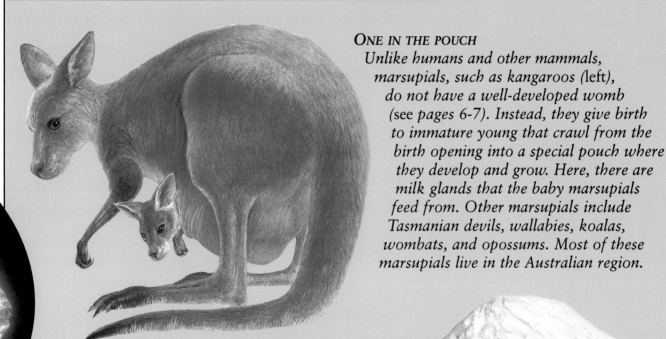

ONE IN THE POUCH
Unlike humans and other mammals, marsupials, such as kangaroos (left), do not have a well-developed womb (see pages 6-7). Instead, they give birth to immature young that crawl from the birth opening into a special pouch where they develop and grow. Here, there are milk glands that the baby marsupials feed from. Other marsupials include Tasmanian devils, wallabies, koalas, wombats, and opossums. Most of these marsupials live in the Australian region.

MAMMALS
Humans, apes, monkeys, cats, dogs, horses, and whales are all mammals and reproduce in the same way. A male and female come together and mate. The babies grow from tiny eggs and develop inside the female's body, in a part called the uterus or womb. After the babies are born, one or both parents look after them, feeding them milk which the mother produces from glands on her body (right).

FEMALE PARTS

THE PARTS OF THE FEMALE BODY involved in producing babies are called the female reproductive system. Two glands called ovaries, found in the lower abdomen region (*left*), make tiny female sex cells, or eggs. These eggs pass along tubes, called the fallopian tubes or oviducts, into the pear-shaped uterus or womb. The opening to the womb is called the cervix and below that lies the vagina (*below*). Once an egg has been fertilized by a male sex cell, it will develop and grow in the lining of the womb.

The production of ripe eggs occurs at regular time intervals or cycles. It is controlled by body chemicals known as sex hormones. These hormones are made mainly in the ovaries and in some parts of the brain.

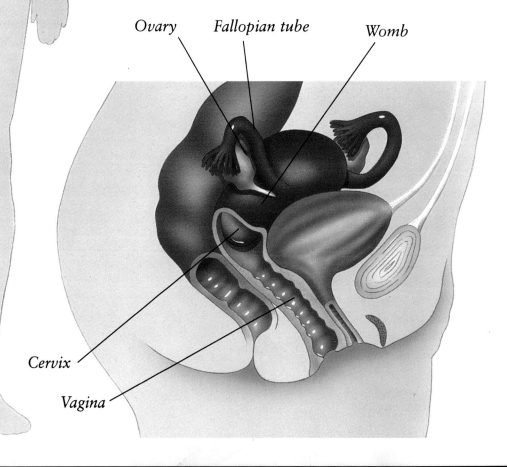

Ovary   *Fallopian tube*   *Womb*

Cervix

Vagina

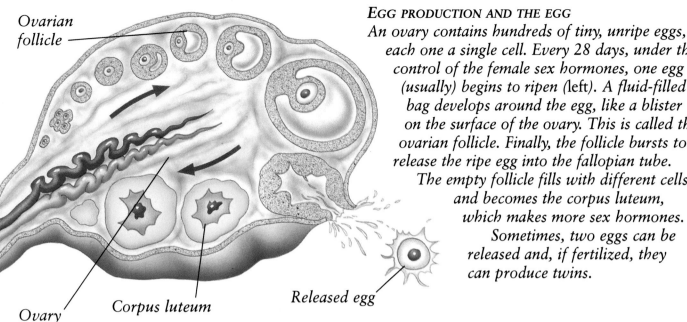

Ovarian
follicle

Ovary

Corpus luteum

Released egg

EGG PRODUCTION AND THE EGG
An ovary contains hundreds of tiny, unripe eggs, each one a single cell. Every 28 days, under the control of the female sex hormones, one egg (usually) begins to ripen (left). A fluid-filled bag develops around the egg, like a blister on the surface of the ovary. This is called the ovarian follicle. Finally, the follicle bursts to release the ripe egg into the fallopian tube. The empty follicle fills with different cells and becomes the corpus luteum, which makes more sex hormones. Sometimes, two eggs can be released and, if fertilized, they can produce twins.

A woman's menstrual cycle continues until egg production stops, a time called menopause. During this time, periods cease and the levels of some sex hormones can decrease. This decrease in hormones can cause emotional distress and physical problems, such as osteoporosis (*see* page 26). To combat these, women can take extra hormones known as Hormone Replacement Therapy (HRT).

INSIDE THE TUBES
The walls of the fallopian tubes are lined with microscopic hairs called cilia (right). These wave back and forth, wafting natural body fluids inside the fallopian tube toward the womb, as well as any released eggs.

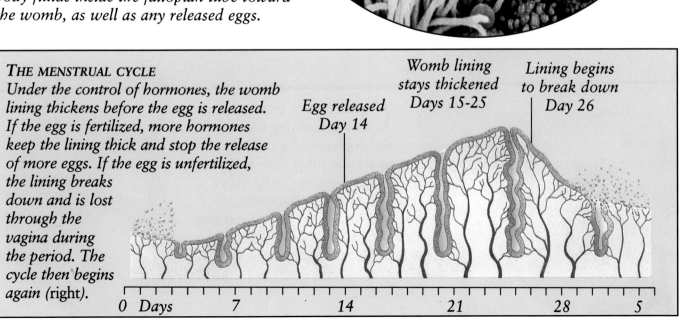

THE MENSTRUAL CYCLE
Under the control of hormones, the womb lining thickens before the egg is released. If the egg is fertilized, more hormones keep the lining thick and stop the release of more eggs. If the egg is unfertilized, the lining breaks down and is lost through the vagina during the period. The cycle then begins again (right).

Egg released
Day 14

Womb lining
stays thickened
Days 15-25

Lining begins
to break down
Day 26

0 Days   7   14   21   28   5

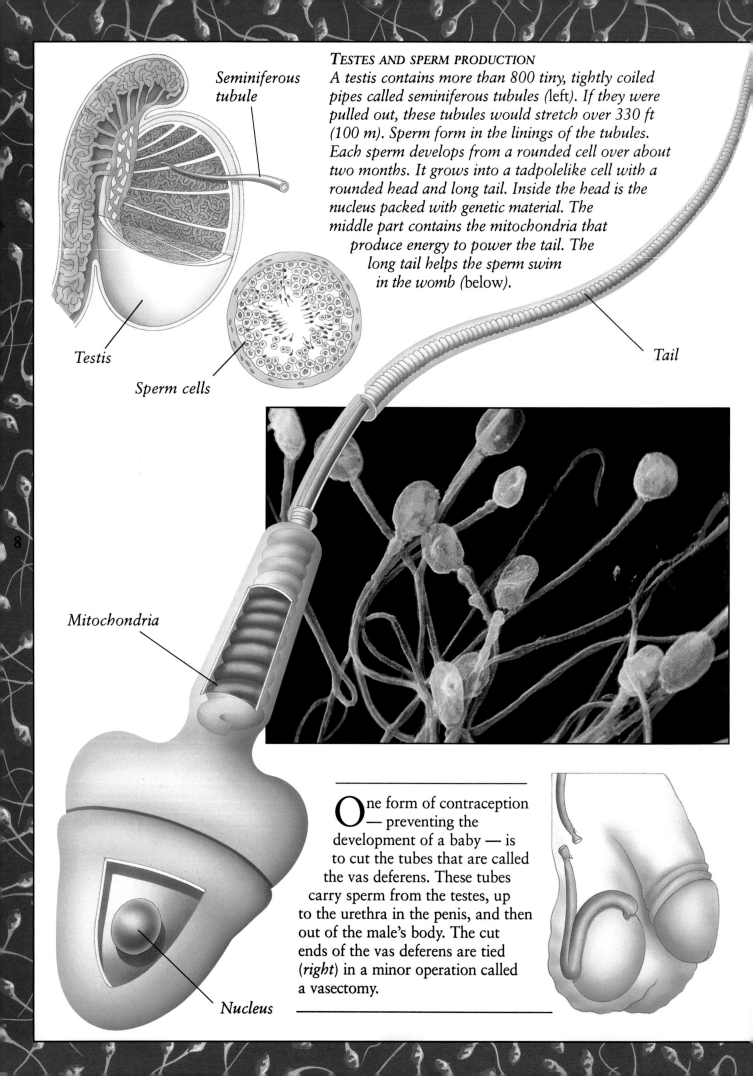

Seminiferous tubule

TESTES AND SPERM PRODUCTION

A testis contains more than 800 tiny, tightly coiled pipes called seminiferous tubules (left). If they were pulled out, these tubules would stretch over 330 ft (100 m). Sperm form in the linings of the tubules. Each sperm develops from a rounded cell over about two months. It grows into a tadpolelike cell with a rounded head and long tail. Inside the head is the nucleus packed with genetic material. The middle part contains the mitochondria that produce energy to power the tail. The long tail helps the sperm swim in the womb (below).

Testis

Sperm cells

Tail

Mitochondria

Nucleus

One form of contraception — preventing the development of a baby — is to cut the tubes that are called the vas deferens. These tubes carry sperm from the testes, up to the urethra in the penis, and then out of the male's body. The cut ends of the vas deferens are tied (*right*) in a minor operation called a vasectomy.

MALE PARTS

THE PARTS OF THE MALE BODY involved in producing babies are called the male reproductive system. Two glands called testes, or testicles, hang between the legs in a bag of skin called the scrotum. Each testis makes the tiny male sex cells called sperm. Unlike the female production of eggs, which happens in a cycle, the production of sperm is continuous. Millions of them develop and become ripe every day, ready to leave the body through the penis. If sperm do not leave, they can be stored for several weeks in a coiled tube, next to each testis, called the epididymis.

PARTS OF THE MALE SYSTEM
The male reproductive system is found in the lower abdomen and between the legs (right). The tube inside the penis, called the urethra (below), is shared with the system that lets a male pass urine.

9

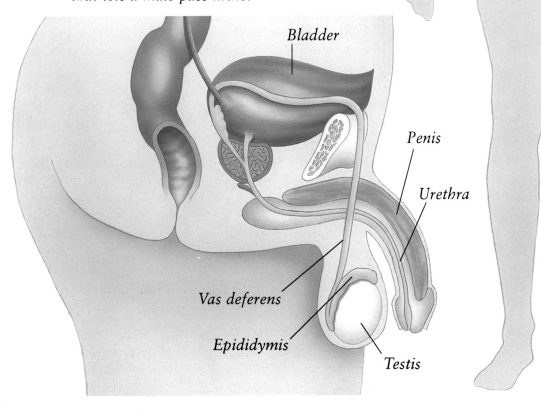

Bladder

Penis

Urethra

Vas deferens

Epididymis

Testis

The EGG and SPERM RACE

A KEY EVENT IN REPRODUCTION is fertilization. This is when the microscopic male and female sex cells, the sperm and the egg, join or fuse together. The sperm contains the genetic material from the father, while the egg contains an equivalent set from the mother. These two come together to produce a new set of genes, from which a new and unique individual will develop.

Fertilization usually takes place in the fallopian tubes. However, it only occurs two or three days after an egg has been released. At other times fertilization cannot happen because there is no egg or the egg is overripe.

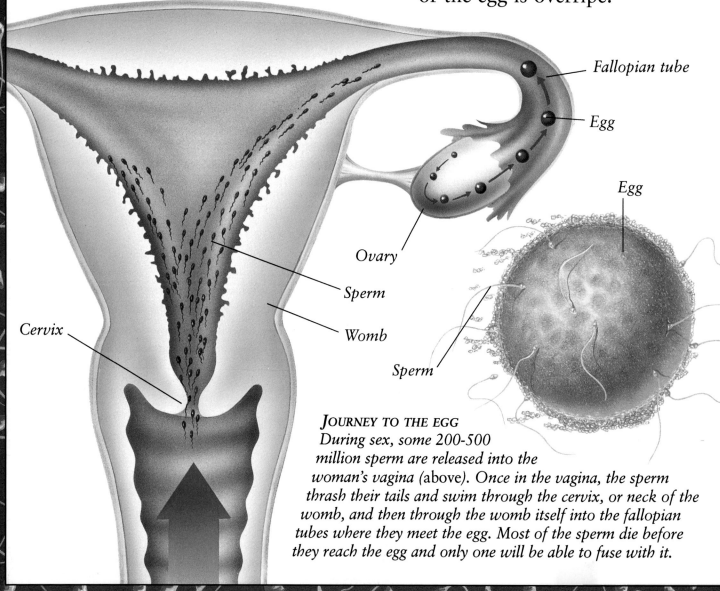

TWINS
Twins are born if two eggs are released from an ovary and both are fertilized, or if one egg splits to form two embryos. If the latter happens, identical twins are born (above).

Fallopian tube

Egg

Egg

Ovary

Sperm

Sperm

Womb

Cervix

JOURNEY TO THE EGG
During sex, some 200-500 million sperm are released into the woman's vagina (above). Once in the vagina, the sperm thrash their tails and swim through the cervix, or neck of the womb, and then through the womb itself into the fallopian tubes where they meet the egg. Most of the sperm die before they reach the egg and only one will be able to fuse with it.

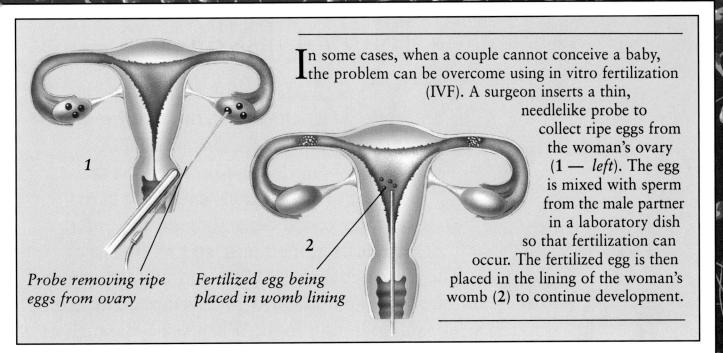

In some cases, when a couple cannot conceive a baby, the problem can be overcome using in vitro fertilization (IVF). A surgeon inserts a thin, needlelike probe to collect ripe eggs from the woman's ovary (**1** — *left*). The egg is mixed with sperm from the male partner in a laboratory dish so that fertilization can occur. The fertilized egg is then placed in the lining of the woman's womb (**2**) to continue development.

1

Probe removing ripe eggs from ovary

2

Fertilized egg being placed in womb lining

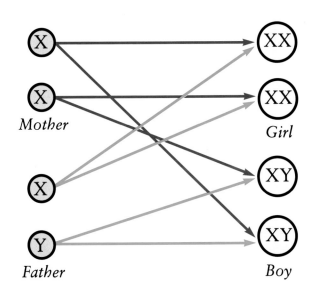

Mother

Father

Girl

Boy

SPERM JOINS EGG

*After sex, thousands of tiny sperm crowd around the much larger egg (**1** — below). The layer or membrane around the head of one sperm merges with the membrane around the egg (**2**). At that point, the nucleus of the sperm enters the egg, leaving behind the middle piece and the tail (**3**). The membrane of the egg then changes to stop any more sperm from entering the egg.*

11

1

Egg membrane

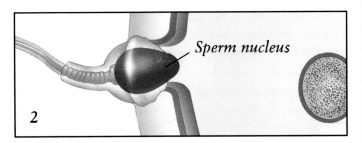

Sperm nucleus

2

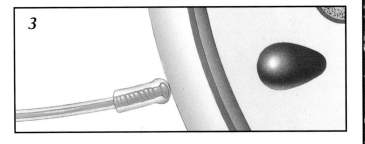

3

BOY OR GIRL?

When the nucleus of the sperm enters the egg, the two nuclei fuse and combine the genetic data that they carry. This genetic data is stored in chromosomes (see pages 12-13). Two types of these chromosomes, known as the "X" and "Y" chromosomes, determine the sex of the child. The fertilized egg cell will get one of these chromosomes from each of the parents — always an X from the mother, but either an X or a Y from the father. If the final mix is two X chromosomes, then the child will be a girl. However, if the two chromosomes are an X and a Y, then the child will be a boy. From the chart (above) you can see that the chances of the child being one sex or the other are exactly equal.

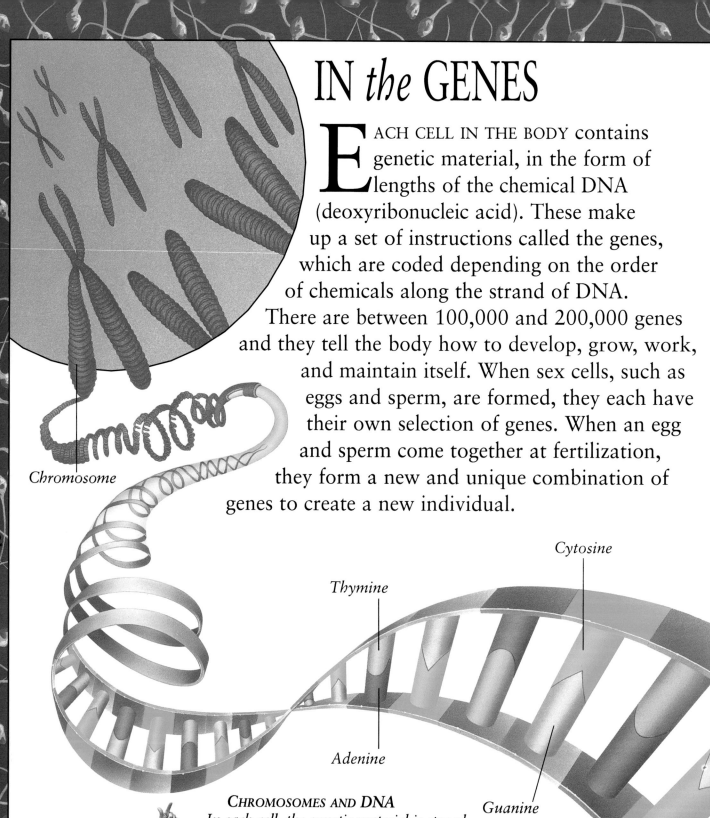

IN *the* GENES

EACH CELL IN THE BODY contains genetic material, in the form of lengths of the chemical DNA (deoxyribonucleic acid). These make up a set of instructions called the genes, which are coded depending on the order of chemicals along the strand of DNA. There are between 100,000 and 200,000 genes and they tell the body how to develop, grow, work, and maintain itself. When sex cells, such as eggs and sperm, are formed, they each have their own selection of genes. When an egg and sperm come together at fertilization, they form a new and unique combination of genes to create a new individual.

12

Chromosome

Thymine

Cytosine

Adenine

Guanine

CHROMOSOMES AND DNA
In each cell, the genetic material is stored in 46 tiny structures called chromosomes (above). Each chromosome consists of a tightly coiled string of DNA. The DNA has sets of four chemicals: thymine, adenine, cytosine, and guanine. These are held together in a twin spiral shape, called a double helix. The order in which these chemicals appear on the DNA strand is the code that tells your body how to develop and grow, giving you, for example, the color of your eyes.

INHERITANCE

Offspring resemble their parents because they receive, or inherit, genetic information from them. But each offspring is a unique individual because he or she receives a different selection of genes from the mother and father. Some recognizable family features, such as hair color or nose shape, are passed from one generation to the next. See if you can create a family tree, like the one on the left, using pictures of your parents and grandparents. Then try to see which physical features have been handed down to you.

MAKING SEX CELLS

Cells divide in your body all the time (right). Normally, when this happens, the genetic material inside copies itself so that the two new cells have a complete set of the 46 chromosomes. This is called mitosis. However, when your body makes sex cells, the genetic information is halved, so that each sex cell only receives 23 chromosomes. This is called meiosis.

Not only does DNA pass on physical characteristics such as the color of your hair, it can pass on certain defects, such as cystic fibrosis and hemophilia. One problem caused by a defect in the genetic information is albinism (*right*). Here, the gene that instructs the body to make the skin-coloring chemical does not work properly. This skin-coloring chemical is called melanin. As a result, a person with albinism has pale skin, pale hair, and can even have pink eyes.

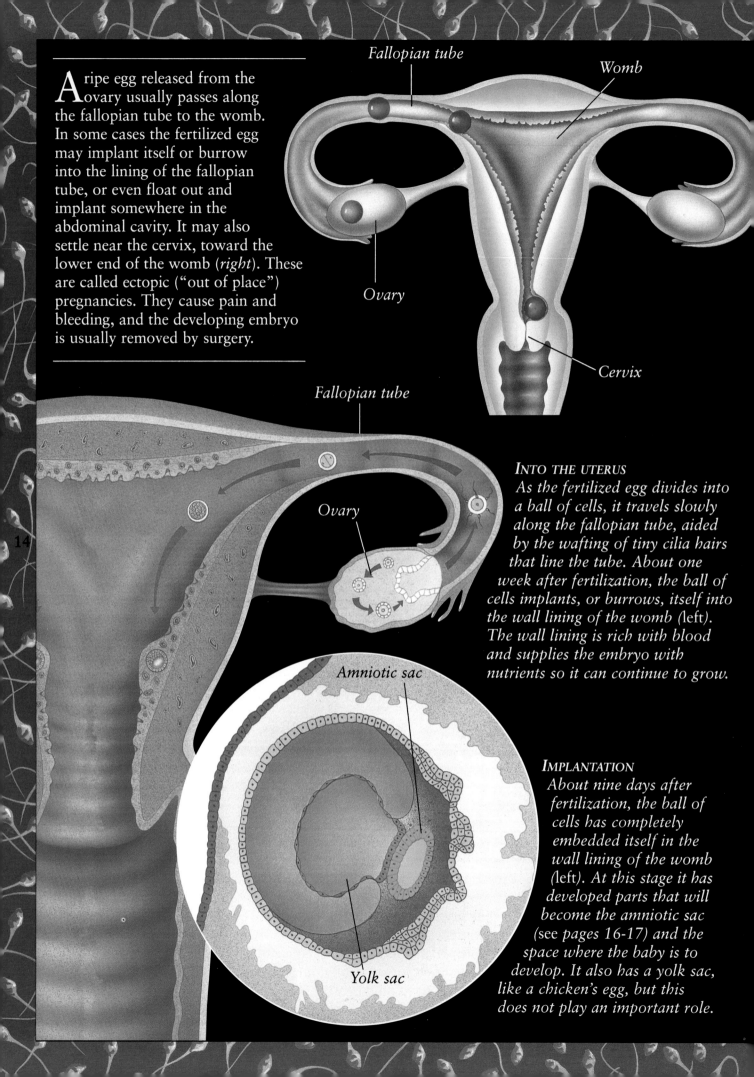

A ripe egg released from the ovary usually passes along the fallopian tube to the womb. In some cases the fertilized egg may implant itself or burrow into the lining of the fallopian tube, or even float out and implant somewhere in the abdominal cavity. It may also settle near the cervix, toward the lower end of the womb (*right*). These are called ectopic ("out of place") pregnancies. They cause pain and bleeding, and the developing embryo is usually removed by surgery.

Fallopian tube

Womb

Ovary

Cervix

Fallopian tube

Ovary

INTO THE UTERUS
As the fertilized egg divides into a ball of cells, it travels slowly along the fallopian tube, aided by the wafting of tiny cilia hairs that line the tube. About one week after fertilization, the ball of cells implants, or burrows, itself into the wall lining of the womb (left). The wall lining is rich with blood and supplies the embryo with nutrients so it can continue to grow.

Amniotic sac

IMPLANTATION
About nine days after fertilization, the ball of cells has completely embedded itself in the wall lining of the womb (left). At this stage it has developed parts that will become the amniotic sac (see pages 16-17) and the space where the baby is to develop. It also has a yolk sac, like a chicken's egg, but this does not play an important role.

Yolk sac

14

The DEVELOPING EMBRYO

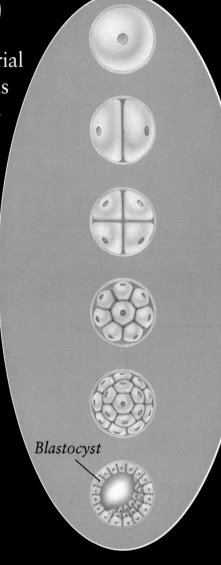

THE FERTILIZED EGG contains all the genetic material required for a new human being to develop. It is also enormous compared to other body cells — about the size of this period. A few hours after fertilization it divides, by splitting in half. A little later, these cells will divide again, and then continue to divide, doubling the number of cells each time (*right*). Within a few days, it has become a tightly packed ball of cells. The cells continue to divide and become different, forming the body parts of the early baby, or embryo as it is called during the first eight weeks of the pregnancy. Over the following weeks, a tiny human body forms. At the same time, the embryo settles on the wall of the womb.

EARLY EMBRYO
The solid mass of cells gradually develops into a hollow ball-shaped structure, called a blastocyst (right). A clump of cells inside the ball will become the baby, while the rest of the cells will form the membranes and other protective layers around the baby.

Blastocyst

15

 *2 weeks*

 3 weeks

DEVELOPMENT OF THE EMBRYO
The clump of cells which makes up the embryo gradually grows larger, curls over at the sides and ends, and develops an inner tube with a bulging end. These will become the baby's spinal cord and brain.

8 weeks

4 weeks

6 weeks

5 weeks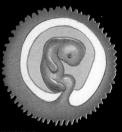

EMBRYO TO FETUS
The arms and legs begin as flaplike buds on the body. The face also takes shape. Eight weeks after fertilization, the baby is the size of your thumb, but it has all of its main body parts (above).

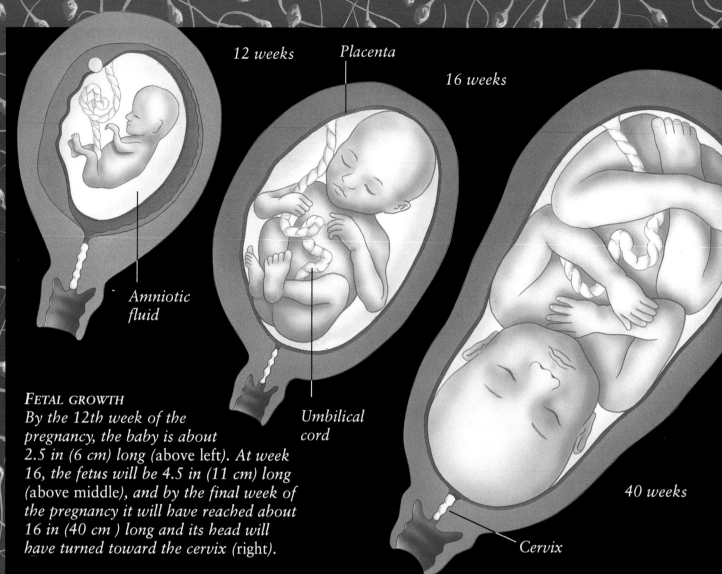

12 weeks   Placenta

16 weeks

Amniotic
fluid

Umbilical
cord

40 weeks

Cervix

FETAL GROWTH
*By the 12th week of the
pregnancy, the baby is about
2.5 in (6 cm) long* (above left). *At week
16, the fetus will be 4.5 in (11 cm) long*
(above middle), *and by the final week of
the pregnancy it will have reached about
16 in (40 cm) long and its head will
have turned toward the cervix (*right).

16

The GROWING FETUS

AFTER THE 8TH WEEK inside the womb, the
unborn baby has developed all of its major
organs and will also have developed its limbs,
including the fingers and toes (although these may still
be joined by webs of skin). The growing child is then
called a fetus. Between this time and the moment of
birth, which occurs about 266 days after fertilization,
the baby will continue to grow and develop its organs.

Throughout this period, the fetus floats inside a
sac filled with amniotic fluid. This liquid acts as a
cushion, protecting the fetus from injury. A special
organ, called the placenta, ensures that the baby
receives all the nutrients it needs.

"SEEING" THE BABY
*Doctors can check on
an unborn child using
ultrasound. Here, a device
sends out very high-pitched
sound waves. These sound
waves "bounce" off the
fetus and are picked up by
a receiver that displays these
echoes on a screen as a
picture of the baby* (below).

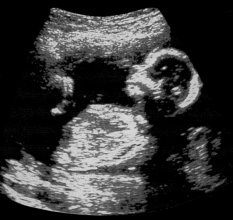

THE PLACENTA

The placenta acts as a temporary link between the unborn child and its mother. Blood from the baby passes down the umbilical cord to the placenta where it enters many fine fingers of tissue, called villi (below). As the baby's blood travels through these villi, nutrients from the mother's blood pass through the walls of the villi and into the baby's blood. The baby's blood then flows through the umbilical cord, back to the child.

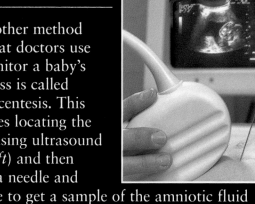

Another method that doctors use to monitor a baby's progress is called amniocentesis. This involves locating the fetus using ultrasound (*see left*) and then using a needle and syringe to get a sample of the amniotic fluid in which the baby floats (*above*). This fluid contains fetal cells and from these cells doctors can extract genetic material (*see* pages 12-13). By examining this genetic material, doctors can find out whether the body will develop any defects, including blood disorders.

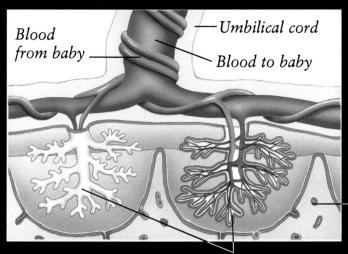

Blood from baby — Umbilical cord — Blood to baby

Villi

Womb lining

SWELLING STOMACH

During the pregnancy, the mother will show a dramatic change in her outward appearance. The "bump" under which the baby is developing first becomes obvious about 16 weeks into the pregnancy (below). By week 36 the top of the womb is level with the woman's ribs. The womb shrinks back to normal around 6 weeks after the birth.

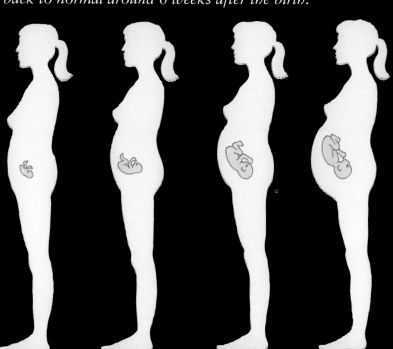

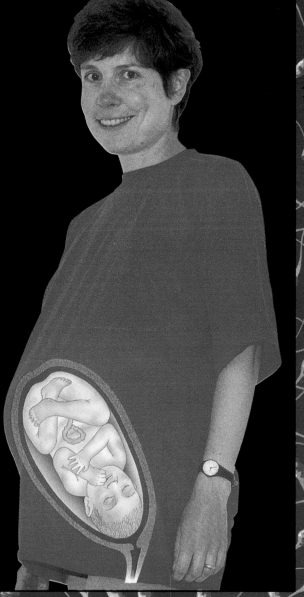

17

BEING BORN

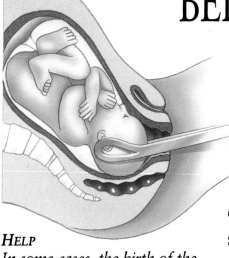

HELP
In some cases, the birth of the baby may require the help of a doctor using a pair of forceps. These are two metal tongs that are placed around the head of the child and are used to ease it out of the womb (above).

D OCTORS ARE STILL UNSURE as to what exactly triggers the moment of birth — some believe it is the child itself, while others think it is the hormone levels in the mother's blood. The amniotic sac around the baby bursts and the amniotic fluid flows out; this is known as the water breaking. At the same time the muscular walls of the womb will contract powerfully to try and push the baby out. The womb neck, or cervix, stretches, or dilates, to about 4 in (10 cm) across. Babies are usually born head first, but sometimes the baby may not be in the right position. Sometimes, it may be delivered by surgery in a caesarean section.

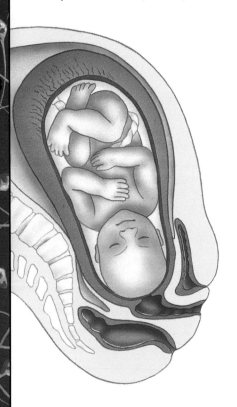

1 ALL GREASED UP
The skin of the baby is covered in a greasy white substance called vernix. It protects the baby from the amniotic fluid and helps the baby's passage through the birth canal as it is being born.

2 HEAD FIRST
As it passes through the birth canal, the baby's head turns to one side to line it up with its shoulders (below).

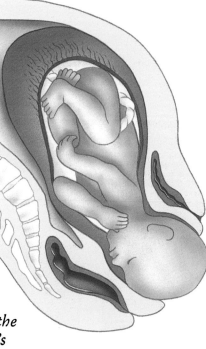

3 OUT IN THE OPEN
As the head appears (below), the birth assistant checks that the umbilical cord is not wrapped around the baby's neck. Fluid is then cleared from the baby's nose and mouth before the shoulders appear.

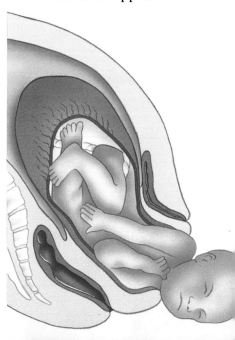

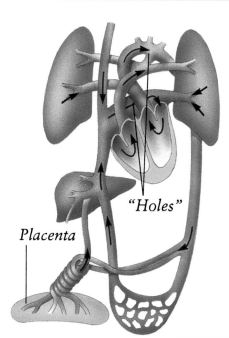

BLOOD SUPPLY IN THE WOMB

In the womb, the baby's lungs are filled with amniotic fluid. Instead of breathing, the baby gets its oxygen through the placenta (left). Two "holes" in the baby's blood circulation, one in the heart and another between two of the blood vessels, divert blood from the baby's lungs.

"Holes"

Placenta

Lungs

OUT OF THE WOMB

At birth, the two "holes" in the baby's bloodstream close (right). This means that the blood flow separates into two systems, one carrying blood to the lungs and the other pushing it to the rest of the body. With the umbilical cord cut, the links that once joined the cord to the baby's blood system soon shrivel.

Sometimes, if a baby has been born prematurely, before the full nine months, or if complications have occurred during the birth, it may have to be cared for in an incubator (*below*). Here, the child is protected from the outside world and doctors can adjust the conditions to suit the baby's needs. The baby may also be put on a respirator. This special machine helps the baby's breathing system to take in air.

4 FINAL STAGES

The rest of the body slides out of the mother and the umbilical cord that used to supply the unborn child with nutrients is cut (above). The child may then cry as it takes its first breaths of air. Soon after the baby has been born, the placenta follows along the birth canal. This is called the afterbirth.

INFANCY

ONCE OUTSIDE the warm comfort of the womb, the human child is bombarded with many experiences and impressions. The baby must now deal with everyday occurrences, such as how it gets its food and how it can gain the attention of its parents. To cope with these, each baby has its own collection of reflexes. These are simple, automatic reactions to outside events that are designed to help the baby throughout this next phase of its life, such as crying, grasping, and suckling.

Before long, the child will also start to learn some of the physical skills that will prove essential in later life, such as handling objects and walking.

CRYING
The first thing a baby does when it emerges from the womb is cry. Crying (above) is a natural reaction that is designed to get the attention of its parents. It also helps to open the baby's airways and lungs, and so make breathing easier.

During the early months of a baby's life, it is important that its health and growth be monitored to make sure that everything is well. Special clinics are usually organized where the baby can be checked and weighed by a doctor or a nurse (*above right*). The baby may also be given vaccinations in these early months to protect against diseases (*see* page 23).

GRABBING HANDS
Newborn babies show a number of reflexes during the first few weeks of their lives. These are known as primitive reflexes. One of these is the grasping reflex. Whenever anything is placed firmly into the palm of the baby, it will automatically grasp and hold on to it (left). Most of these primitive reflexes normally disappear after the first couple of months.

BREAST FEEDING

Another common baby reflex is the rooting reflex. Whenever the corner of a baby's mouth is lightly touched it will turn its head and open its mouth. This reflex helps the baby to find the mother's nipple when breast feeding (right). New mothers produce milk in special glands in their breasts. The mother's milk contains nutrients that are vital for the baby, including sugars such as lactose, fats, and minerals (below).

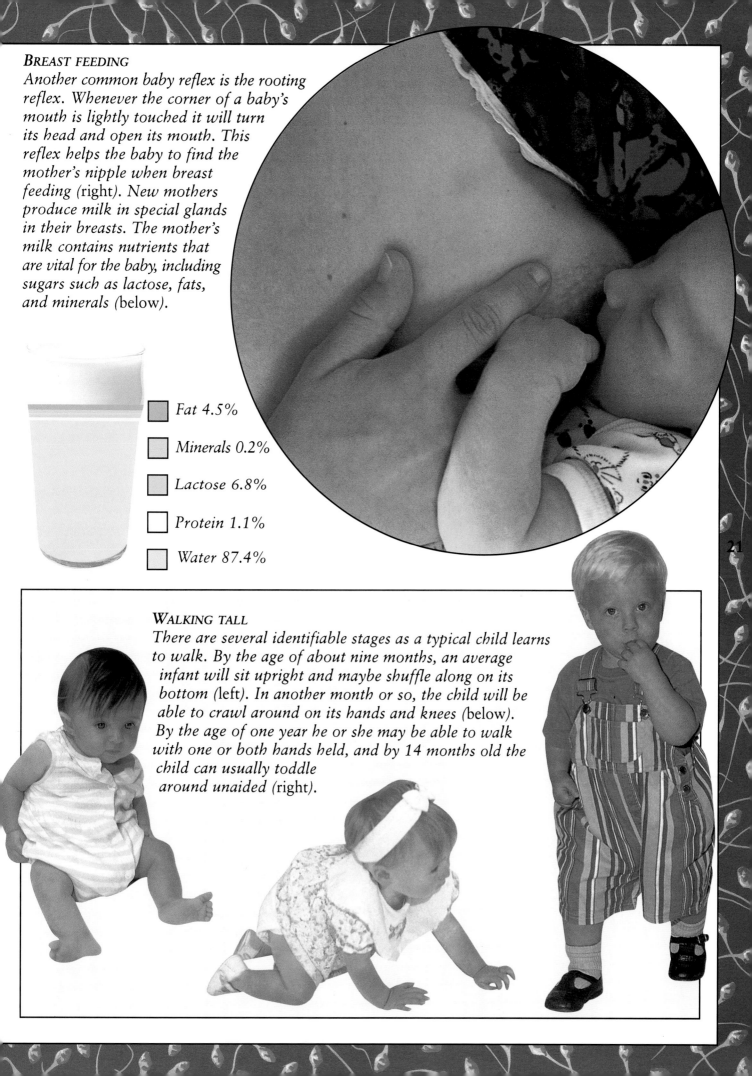

Fat 4.5%

Minerals 0.2%

Lactose 6.8%

Protein 1.1%

Water 87.4%

WALKING TALL

There are several identifiable stages as a typical child learns to walk. By the age of about nine months, an average infant will sit upright and maybe shuffle along on its bottom (left). In another month or so, the child will be able to crawl around on its hands and knees (below). By the age of one year he or she may be able to walk with one or both hands held, and by 14 months old the child can usually toddle around unaided (right).

CHILDHOOD

T HE PERIOD OF INFANCY and childhood, until the time of puberty (*see* pages 24-25), is one of almost constant learning. During this time you learn to talk, read, write, communicate with others and feed yourself, as well as a whole host of other skills, from riding a bike to maybe even in-line skating (*above right*).

Also during this period, your body grows. During the first 18 months of your life, your body grew very quickly, but after that growth slowed to a more steady pace. There is another growth spurt at the time of puberty.

TALKING
Scientists are unsure as to why a child starts to talk. Some believe that an area in the brain is already programmed with a basic ability to communicate, while others think that babies pick up the use of language by listening to others (above).

READING AND WRITING
Both reading and writing skills benefit from skilled teaching, usually at school with the use of books (right).

BODY DIMENSIONS
Compare these three pictures (right) *of a baby, an infant and a child. You will see that the proportions of parts of their bodies differ. In a baby, the head is very large when compared to the rest of its body which has very short arms and legs. All the parts grow, but the head appears to reduce in size when compared to the rest of the body, while the limbs become relatively longer.*

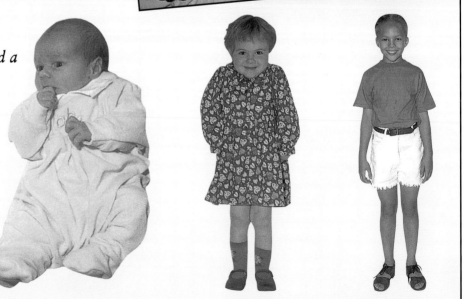

PLAYING AND LEARNING
Early childhood is a time when you learn to interact with other people, especially with those of the same age. In preschool groups and then in school (right) you will be able to play and learn with others. All the time you develop communication and socializing skills that will become vital in later life.

To help protect you from infectious diseases, such as polio and tetanus, most children receive vaccinations (*left*). Some of these vaccinations contain weakened forms of the disease that will not do any harm. Once inside your body, your immune defense system will recognize the vaccination as a foreign object and attack it. It will then memorize the makeup of the disease. In the future, your defense system will be able to recognize the harmful form of the disease should it infect you. It can then destroy the disease quickly.

LEARNING SKILLS
Early childhood is also a time when you learn many physical or motor skills. As you grow older, you gain greater control over your body and you will be able to undertake more complicated activities. Riding a bike (left), for example, involves balancing your body weight on two narrow wheels and coordinating the movements of your feet on the pedals and your hands on the handlebars.

23

GROWING UP

DURING THE EARLY teenage years, a time called puberty, your body will undergo some very dramatic changes as it becomes sexually mature. Some of these changes may occur suddenly, while others happen more gradually. Girls might notice their breasts swell, while boys might notice their voice starting to crack. Both sexes may also feel emotional upheavals that are caused by changes in body chemistry. The time of emotional and social development, which includes the physical changes of puberty, is called adolescence.

24

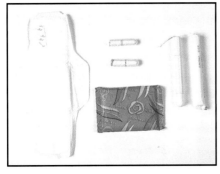

When a girl begins her periods (see pages 6-7), she usually uses one of a wide range of sanitary products (above). These include sanitary pads, which can be stuck to ordinary pants, or tampons, which can be used with or without applicators.

FEMALE MATURITY
On average, girls go through the stages of puberty about two years before boys. Perhaps the most noticeable change is the beginning of periods, a time called menarche. The average age for menarche is between 11 and 13 years. An increase of chemicals, called sex hormones, in the body will also bring about hair growth around the genitals and under the armpits. Meanwhile, girls also experience a change in body shape, as hips and shoulders become more rounded.

STRENGTH AND SPEED

Throughout childhood there is little difference in the athletic performance of boys and girls — their body shapes remain similar during these early years. However, when boys reach puberty their muscles begin to enlarge and become stronger than girls', while the fat content of their bodies begins to decline. As a result, the average man is stronger and faster than the average woman. But there is a great range in strength, with a lot of overlapping between the sexes.

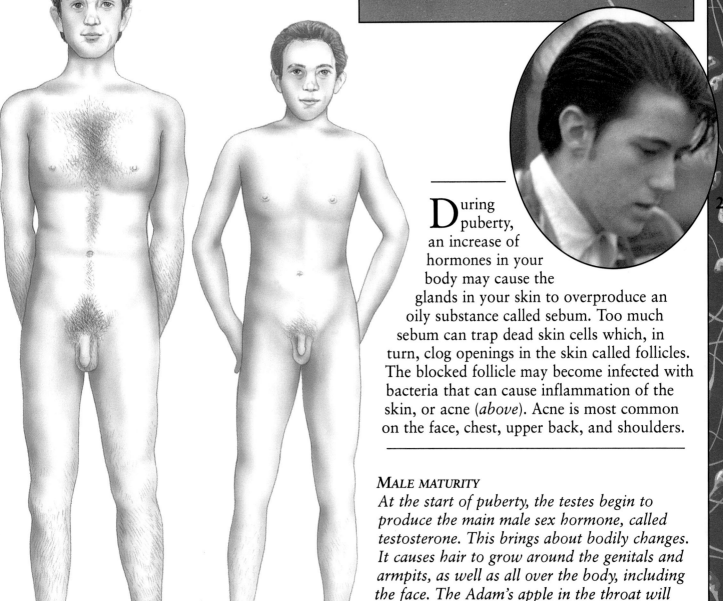

D uring puberty, an increase of hormones in your body may cause the glands in your skin to overproduce an oily substance called sebum. Too much sebum can trap dead skin cells which, in turn, clog openings in the skin called follicles. The blocked follicle may become infected with bacteria that can cause inflammation of the skin, or acne (*above*). Acne is most common on the face, chest, upper back, and shoulders.

MALE MATURITY

At the start of puberty, the testes begin to produce the main male sex hormone, called testosterone. This brings about bodily changes. It causes hair to grow around the genitals and armpits, as well as all over the body, including the face. The Adam's apple in the throat will get larger and the voice will crack, or get deeper. Testosterone also encourages body muscle to grow (see above) and will make the testes start to produce sperm.

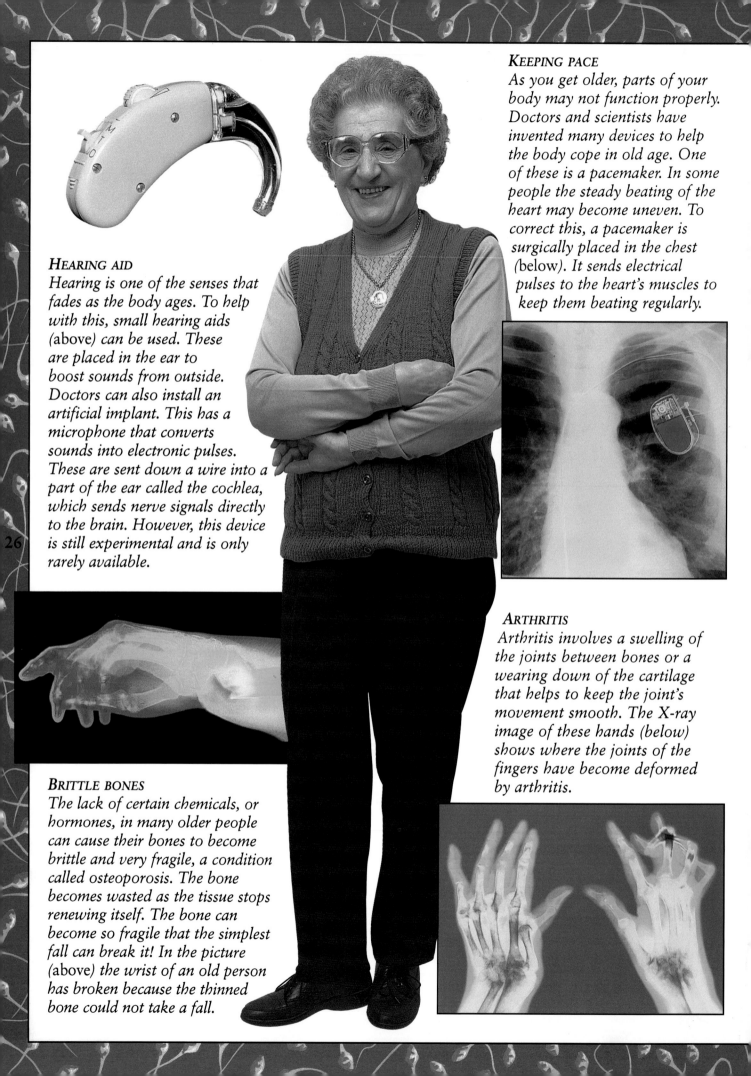

KEEPING PACE
As you get older, parts of your body may not function properly. Doctors and scientists have invented many devices to help the body cope in old age. One of these is a pacemaker. In some people the steady beating of the heart may become uneven. To correct this, a pacemaker is surgically placed in the chest (below). It sends electrical pulses to the heart's muscles to keep them beating regularly.

HEARING AID
Hearing is one of the senses that fades as the body ages. To help with this, small hearing aids (above) can be used. These are placed in the ear to boost sounds from outside. Doctors can also install an artificial implant. This has a microphone that converts sounds into electronic pulses. These are sent down a wire into a part of the ear called the cochlea, which sends nerve signals directly to the brain. However, this device is still experimental and is only rarely available.

ARTHRITIS
Arthritis involves a swelling of the joints between bones or a wearing down of the cartilage that helps to keep the joint's movement smooth. The X-ray image of these hands (below) shows where the joints of the fingers have become deformed by arthritis.

BRITTLE BONES
The lack of certain chemicals, or hormones, in many older people can cause their bones to become brittle and very fragile, a condition called osteoporosis. The bone becomes wasted as the tissue stops renewing itself. The bone can become so fragile that the simplest fall can break it! In the picture (above) the wrist of an old person has broken because the thinned bone could not take a fall.

The AGING BODY

After you reach maturity, when you have grown to your full height, usually around the age of 20, parts of your body will start to get old. Many of its systems will begin to decline even at this early age. It may be many years before their effects become visible, and then it is only obvious effects that you can see, such as gray hair, wrinkled skin, or a stooped appearance. These conditions may only become apparent between the ages of 45 to 55.

Exactly when these aging processes start and how fast they progress depends on many things. These include the genetic information stored in the cells, the health of the body, and the conditions that it has experienced throughout its lifetime.

Part of the aging process is the death of cells, called apoptosis. Special genes in the cell nucleus tell the cell when it is time to die. When this happens the cell falls apart and is absorbed into your body. Compare the living cell (*above top*) with the cell that has just died (*above below*). This process occurs in your body every day.

LIFE EXPECTANCY
How long you live is determined by a great many things. One of these can be the conditions in which you live. A person living in a rich country (left) *where food and health care are plentiful can expect to live, on average, over 70 years. Alternatively, a person who lives in a poorer country* (above), *where health care and nutrition are not of the same standard, can expect to live for just over 50 years. However, the comforts of a richer way of life can have their own drawbacks. People who live in wealthier countries suffer more from obesity and heart disease than those in poorer countries.*

INFERTILITY
and CONTRACEPTION

S OME PEOPLE may have difficulty in conceiving a baby. They may have a defective reproductive system that produces malformed sex cells (*see right*). Alternatively, their lifestyle or previous health problems, such as an abdominal infection, may have damaged their reproductive system. In many cases these problems can be corrected by fertility treatments, such as IVF (*see* page 11).

Other people may not want to have a baby at the moment. They can use several methods to stop a baby from being conceived, called contraception. These can include the female oral pill. This alters the hormones in the body to simulate a pregnancy, which, in turn, stops the release of any more eggs from the ovaries. Other forms of contraception include condoms (*see right*).

STRESS
The pressures of modern life can affect the ability of a couple to conceive a baby (above). Stress, worry, and anxiety affect levels of body hormones. These varying hormonal levels can disrupt the reproductive system and affect the making of sperm and the release of eggs into the fallopian tubes.

28

DRUGS AND FERTILITY
Certain drugs, such as nicotine in cigarettes (left), affect the sex organs and may cause temporary infertility. Some prescribed or medicinal drugs do this as a side-effect, and a doctor can advise on this and suggest alternatives. The persistent misuse or abuse of illegal drugs (right) is another possible cause of infertility. Their damaging effects on the reproductive system and the baby are increased by chemicals that are added to the drugs when they are manufactured.

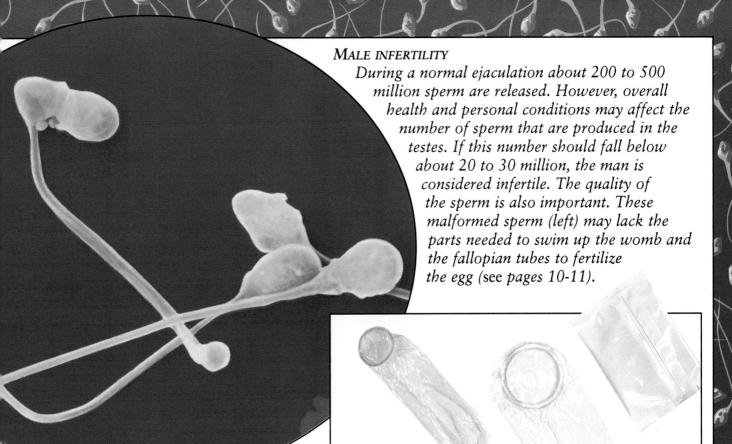

MALE INFERTILITY

During a normal ejaculation about 200 to 500 million sperm are released. However, overall health and personal conditions may affect the number of sperm that are produced in the testes. If this number should fall below about 20 to 30 million, the man is considered infertile. The quality of the sperm is also important. These malformed sperm (left) may lack the parts needed to swim up the womb and the fallopian tubes to fertilize the egg (see pages 10-11).

CONTRACEPTIVES

There are many forms of contraception available that range in effectiveness. Condoms (right) can be used by both men and women. They work by trapping the sperm and so preventing them from entering the womb and swimming to reach the egg.

Scientists have now developed a way of copying, or cloning, an adult animal — previously it was only possible from the cells of an embryo. By taking cells from the adult animal and extracting the DNA (*see* pages 12-13) the scientists can then implant this DNA into the growing cells of an embryo. As this embryo grows it will become an exact genetic replica of the adult that the DNA was taken from. The first animal to be cloned from the cells of an adult was a sheep, called Dolly (*right*). Cloning has created controversy around the world, and many countries have banned the cloning of cells, especially human ones.

KNOW YOUR BODY!

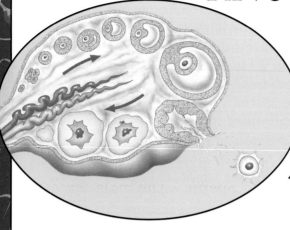

DURING HER LIFETIME, *a woman will release no more than between 400 and 500 eggs from her ovaries (left). However, when she is born, her ovaries will contain a great many more — between 400,000 and 800,000 eggs!*

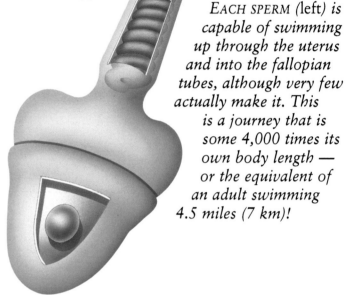

EACH SPERM *(left) is capable of swimming up through the uterus and into the fallopian tubes, although very few actually make it. This is a journey that is some 4,000 times its own body length — or the equivalent of an adult swimming 4.5 miles (7 km)!*

THE TESTES IN THE SCROTUM *(below) are kept at a temperature 3° F cooler than the rest of the body. This allows maximum sperm production. In warm temperatures, the skin of the scrotum hangs loosely and the testes are held in a lower position. In cold temperatures, muscles under the skin of the scrotum contract and pull the testes closer to the body.*

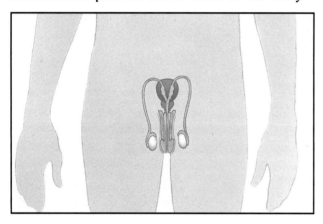

THE OLDEST *authenticated human was Jeanne Louis Calment (left). She was born in France on February 21, 1875, and died over 122 years later in 1997.*

THE GREATEST NUMBER *of children born at a single birth stands at ten. They were born at Baracay in Brazil in 1946. The greatest number of children born to one mother is 69, by Feodor Vassilyev from Russia. These included 16 pairs of twins, seven sets of triplets, and four sets of quadruplets!*

GLOSSARY

Amniocentesis – The sampling of cells from the amniotic fluid using a long needle and a syringe.

Amniotic fluid – A clear fluid that is contained inside the amniotic sac. It acts as a buffer to protect the baby from any bumps.

Amniotic sac – A tough, thin, and transparent membrane around the developing baby.

Apoptosis – The death of a cell. It is controlled by so-called "cell-death genes" that are contained within the cell's nucleus.

Chromosome – A tiny structure found in every cell's nucleus. It contains the genetic information for that creature, stored in a tightly coiled chain of a chemical called DNA. Each human cell has 46 chromosomes, except for the sex cells that only have 23.

Corpus luteum – The name given to the ovarian follicle after the ripe egg has been released.

DNA (deoxyribonucleic acid) – The long chemical that holds the genetic information in special coded sequences.

Embryo – A name given to the unborn child until the 8th week of the pregnancy.

Epididymis – A tightly coiled tube that sits alongside each testis. It stores excess sperm and also carries them from the testes into the vas deferens.

Fallopian tubes – The tubes that lead from the ovaries to the womb. The eggs are carried along them after they have been released from an ovary.

Fetus – The name given to the unborn baby eight weeks after fertilization and until birth.

Genes – A segment of DNA that controls a particular function. Certain genes are passed down from generation to generation.

Hormone – A chemical "messenger." Hormones are produced by special glands in the body and control the rate at which parts of the body work.

Labor – The pain and effort associated with giving birth to a child.

Ovarian follicle – The fluid-filled bag that forms around the egg as it ripens in the ovary.

Ovaries – The female sex organs. These produce the female sex cells, called eggs, releasing them into the fallopian tubes where they can be fertilized by the male sex cells, called sperm.

Sperm – The male sex cells. These tadpole-shaped cells are produced in the testes that hang in the saclike scrotum found between the male's legs.

Testes – Parts of the male reproductive system. They are kept cooler than the rest of the body by hanging in a sac, called the scrotum.

Ultrasound – A method of "seeing" an unborn baby using soundwaves that are too high-pitched to hear. These sound waves bounce off the baby and the echoes are picked up by an ultrasound scanner. The results are then displayed on a screen.

Uterus – A hollow, pear-shaped organ that sits behind the woman's bladder. It holds the developing baby and is also called the womb.

Vas deferens – The tubes that carry sperm from the epididymis into the urethra that runs inside the penis.

INDEX

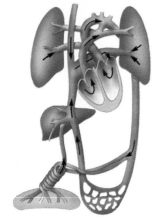

Photo credits:
    Abbreviations: t-top, m-middle, b-bottom, r-right, l-left

All the photographs in this book are by Roger Vlitos except the following pages:

Front cover l, pages 4, 7, 8, 13m, 16, 17t, 23tl, 26t, mr, bl & br, 27t, & 29t — Science Photo Library. 10, 13b, 19 both, 20m, 21t, 29b, & 30 — Frank Spooner Pictures. 27bl — Paul Nightingale. 27br — Solution Pictures.